The Gift of Rudy

The Gift of Rudy
©2018 Sharon Ruchman

Published by Spuyten Duyvil
An imprint of Hobo Jungle Press
Sharon, Connecticut, USA
St. Vincent & the Grenadines

Printed in the United States of America

All rights reserved. No part of this publication may be reproduced, distributed, or transmitted in any form or by any means, including photocopying, recording, or other electronic or mechanical methods, without the prior written permission of the publisher, except in the case of brief quotations embodied in critical reviews and certain other noncommercial uses permitted by copyright law.

ISBN # 9781730919077

An audio version of *Another Time* can be downloaded at thegiftofrudy.com

Cover art: *Dan Hamilton*

The Gift of Rudy

Sharon Ruchman

Table of Contents

Introduction	7
Prelude	8
Lachrymose (mournful, causing tears)	9
Prima (leading)	15
Secondo (second)	16
Discordance (strife)	18
Dissonance (conflict, lack of harmony)	23
Giocoso (joyful)	25
Con Dolore (with sadness)	28
Consonance (agreement, compatibility)	34
Timorose (with hesitation)	41
Inquieto (restless, uneasy)	42
Risoluto (bold, resolved)	44
Fermato (firmly resolute)	45
Sonore (harmonious)	48
Apassionato (with fervor)	49
Ardore (with love and warmth)	51
Misterioso (mysterious)	54
Fastoso y Con Amore (proudly and with love)	56
Coda (finale)	58
The Soul of Music	59
Another Time (musical score)	60
Acknowledgements	64
Bio of Sharon Ruchman	65
Bio of Rudy	67

Introduction

It was only a few years ago, 2016, when I began the search for someone to write my great uncle's remarkable story. I didn't feel equipped to handle a book project, lacking the confidence in my writing skills.

I wanted to tell the story, but wasn't certain who would be the best person to relate it. Last September 2017, at the local post office, I ran into Davyne Verstandig, a writing consultant who helped my friend with his memoir. We scheduled a breakfast meeting a few days later to discuss my intention. Davyne thought that Rudy's story was an extraordinary one, suggesting that I should be the one to tell it.

I came to the realization that Rudy's love of music and his family had a strong connection to me, and that I also needed to share my story. In October I began writing. This was a momentous turning point in my life — facing the past — but also discovering much about the present through new explorations of music and writing.

The journey with Rudy began over 25 years ago when I received his stack of violin sheet music, later accepting his gifts of letters, a viola, a recording, recital programs, and photos. These opened up opportunities for me. The thrill of playing his viola, the adventures of writing, experiencing the joy of composing, has been deeply satisfying and fulfilling.

It is Rudy, a man I never met, and his story, that have helped me develop into someone who acknowledges and recognizes my creative accomplishments and my abilities. For all of this I am extremely grateful.

Prelude

My initial experience as a writer felt like being in a dark and strange place, unable to see where the path would lead, where or what I would find. The process of writing has become illuminating and challenging. By allowing myself the freedom to be honest and forthright, unafraid to explore inner thoughts and feelings, I have faced hard truths about my past.

As I write with deep interest about my great uncle Rudy and his story, I recognize his life — filled with love of music and family — parallels mine. It is this journey of our lives intertwining that has inspired me to write a memoir.

What began as an inquiry led to my discovery of writing and playing the viola, both of which give my life richness and contentment. In the past I often shied away from something unknown, feeling uncomfortable about my abilities to achieve my goals. I am now pushing those boundaries without restraint as I find out where this story will take me. This unexpected journey is transforming my life.

Fuchs family Passover Seder, 1933. Top row (l to r) Henry Fuchs, Rudy Fuchs, Cousin Gert, Morris Fuchs, Raymond Fuchs, Joe Fuchs, Jules Singer, Charles Fuchs, Kenneth Fuchs, and Leon Singer. Bottom row (l to r) Jerry Fuchs, Stella (Kominsky) Fuchs, Minnie Singer, Sally Fuchs, "Grandma" Rose Fuchs, "Grandpa" Sam Fuchs, Jeanette Fuchs, and Mr. and Mrs. Levy (parents of Jeanette Fuchs).

Lachrymose *(mournful, causing tears)*

In April 1933, when Rudy was a concert master on a radio station in Los Angeles, he drove his recently purchased car to Brooklyn, New York, to join his parents and siblings for a Passover Seder. It was a long drive, one that he insisted on taking. The Seder was at the family's old, but elegant apartment.

Rudy was a special member of the family, loved and admired by them as well as his music colleagues. He was not only a caring and generous person, but was considered by critics and musicians alike as one of the finest younger musicians of his generation.

Rudy stayed on until June when he received a telegram from Albert Vertchamp, his violin teacher, with whom he played in the same string quartet. Albert urged Rudy to leave immediately for Los Angeles to play an important gig. Sam — Rudy's father — who felt the trip would be too long and taxing for him, encouraged him to take the train back to the West Coast and leave his car in New York. Rudy agreed, purchased a train ticket and set off to California, first having a fairly long layover in Chicago, the site of the World's Fair.

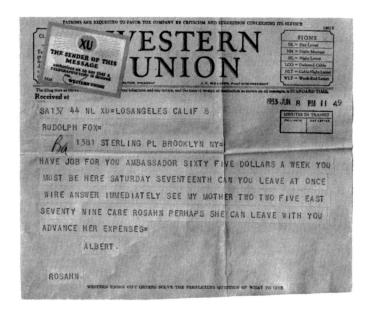

The 1933 Chicago World's Fair ("Century of Progress" International Exposition) had 22 million visitors from all over the world. It was a time of optimism even though the country was witnessing the Great Depression.

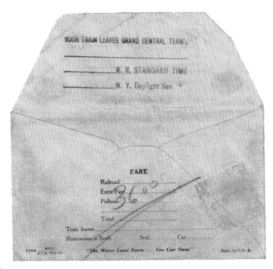

When Rudy's train had a layover in Chicago he must have felt like a kid in a candy store, elated at being there, seizing an opportunity to see as much of the Fair as possible in the short time he had before he train departed for Los Angeles. It must have been like nothing Rudy could ever have imagined, so alluring that he would even consider checking his rare and precious violin — his appendage — into a locker. Although there were sky rides to see the sights above ground, the best way to get an overview of the exposition was from a Sikorsky sea plane, offering passengers the experience to see it all. Its interior looked like a lounge with comfortable seating, plush chairs and a window bench for ten, including storage areas for belongings — certainly far more luxurious than one would expect from a sightseeing plane. It beckoned Rudy, a once-in-a-lifetime experience that he couldn't pass up.

IMPORTANT FEATURES OF THE S-38

The SIKORSKY AMPHIBION is built of the best materials obtainable, by skilled workmen who know structural methods. Its frame, constructed almost entirely of duralumin, a material nearly as strong as steel and as light as aluminum, possesses tremendous strength and durability which enables it to meet the severest strains.

The method of construction is unusual for airplanes, since welding is entirely avoided. The open sections, of substantial thickness, are riveted and bolted together, just as in steel structures such as bridges an skyscrapers.

Passengers find relaxation and comfort in the roomy cabin. They can converse in ordinary tones, play bridge if they like and smoke when they choose. A safe fuel supply passes directly from the upper wing to the motors without passing through the cabin, which is thus entirely free from gasoline fumes and the danger of fire.

The cabin is well ventilated, electrically lighted and comfortably furnished. The entrance is from a hatchway on top, an arrangement superior to the use of a side entrance door, because it permits opening the sliding top while in the air and even on a rough sea.

Looking through non-shatterable glass windows, passengers have an unobstructed view of the country below. As the engines are separate from the hull and cabin the plane is remarkably free from vibration and noise.

From a brochure highlighting the features of the Sikorsky S-38.

Chicago Tribune headline following the crash of Sikorsky S-38 on June 11, 1933

The Gift of Rudy

A scrapbook page saved by a family member

According to newspaper reports at the time, the amphibious plane was crippled in flight and attempted unsuccessfully to land in the choppy waters of Lake Michigan. Ultimately, it crashed in the nearby town of Glenview. When news of the crash was reported, there was utter disbelief, shock and despair. Rudy's death was unbearable to the family. They never imagined that a man of such enormous talent and kindness, the most gifted of all of his siblings, could lose his life at the young age of 25. No one ever fully recovered, the wounds too deep. Violin music would cease in that household.

Each family member was affected differently. Rudy's father would die within a year of a broken heart, his guilt too great after advising Rudy to return to Los Angeles by train instead of driving back.

Charlie, Rudy's older brother, also a violinist, kept Rudy's violin after the crash, eventually selling it. Charlie saved every document, recital program and photo of Rudy, a testament to his deep love and regard for him. My father, only 12 years old at the time of the crash, was greatly impacted by the absence of his uncle, missing the days when he listened to Rudy practice Brahms' *Hungarian Rhapsody #5 in F# minor,* a melody that stayed embedded in his memory, and that he often hummed to me.

Prima (leading)

I was born in Brooklyn, New York, August 7, 1949, my mom telling me years later that it was one of the hottest days that summer. In 1951 we moved to Far Rockaway, Queens, living in one of the "Projects," which were rent controlled apartment buildings.

My parents often made movies of my brother and me. In one movie, made in front of my apartment building, friends were jumping from a wooden bench, the seat a few feet above the sidewalk. When it was my turn to jump, I saw myself looking timid and reluctant to make the move. When I finally did jump, a huge smile came across my face, as if I accomplished something monumental. It reminds me of my experiences in high school gym classes where I couldn't round up the courage to climb the ropes or jump over the wooden horse, always stopping shy of it for fear of getting hurt or feeling unable to master it.

Secondo (second)

When I was five years old we moved from the projects in Far Rockaway to the second floor of a modest, grey-shingled, two-story home in Kingston, New York, about three hours north of New York City.

In the living room I sat on an embroidered piano bench at a baby grand piano given to us by my grandmother. The piano seemed to have taken most of the space in the cramped room. I remember the delight I felt exploring the range of piano keys and the possibilities of sounds each offered me. Sitting at the piano every day I started to create little melodies. When I began taking lessons at age 8, I learned basic theory. My first piece was entitled *The Wind*, with original lyrics, notes properly situated on the staff and bar lines, although the time signature was missing. I still have the manuscript book to this day.

In 1957 I began formal piano lessons with a young, amiable piano teacher who lived a few blocks from me. My mother and I would walk together to her white, colonial style home where I had my morning lessons. Miss Altamarie had an elegant and grand living room with a black and white tiled floor. I remember being dazzled by her beautiful ebony grand pianos used for playing duets with her students. Learning the piano came easily to me; I enjoyed my teacher who had a wonderful disposition, encouraging me in my studies.

My elementary school was nearby so when the opportunity arose to learn the cello at school I decided to take lessons. My memory is rather hazy, but I do remember my mother meeting me on my way home from school with a heavy metal wagon to transport the cello to our house. She seemed to be puzzled as to why I would choose to play an instrument almost as big as I was.

I was involved in several activities at school, including singing and dancing as well as sports. There was a local dance studio where my brother and I learned tap dancing; we performed in several recitals. The dance productions were quite elaborate with flashy costumes. I wore everything from a tuxedo jacket printed with music notes on it and a top hat, to a light pink, sequined mermaid costume with aqua-colored netting at the bottom of it; or being Miss Daisy May with a straw hat and a daisy sticking out of it. My brother also performed posing as Neptune. Our lives then were full of activities: sledding and ice skating during the cold and snowy winters, roller skating on uneven sidewalks after school, or stopping by the candy store down the street and treating ourselves to Popsicles. Our biggest thrill was going to Babcock's on a warm summer's night, where we would enjoy licking our ice cream cones, stacked two or three scoops high. My favorite flavors were pistachio, mint chocolate chip, and raspberry.

Our family trips included places such as Sleepy Hollow, Howe Caverns and Niagara Falls, or vacations in the Catskills. On occasion, we would stop by local antique stores where my father, a collector, looked for old postcards and stamps.

Our elderly neighbors, Miss Dodge and Miss Rich, sisters and widows, were very friendly and had a great interest in gardening. They often showed off their flowers. My favorite was a beautiful, deep blue morning glory.

Miss Castor, at the end of the street, was also a widow and often babysat us. She lived in one room with barely a possession or food to eat. When I dropped by to visit her, she managed to offer me a cup of tea with a biscuit. I saw her often because I enjoyed her stories and her company. On a shelf was a photo of her daughter, an opera singer, of whom she was very proud.

Life was not fancy in our town, but it was rich in many ways.

Discordance (*strife*)

I moved to Long Island — a more prosperous area than Kingston — in 1959 when I was ten years old and ready to enter fifth grade. My parents believed that moving to Long Island was a step up from where we lived before, allowing my brother and me to have a better education and more Jewish life. The cultural contrast was stark from the small town of Kingston where life was simple and less stressful. During the eleven years I lived there, I never felt I belonged.

Although I excelled in school in Kingston, I was not placed in an honors class in my new school. It was a huge disappointment for me, adding to my insecurities. There were pressures and expectations, especially for material things. Many of my friends went to sleep-away camp and purchased their clothing at high-end stores. I was self-conscious, for example, when asked by a classmate where I bought my shoes.

As a teenager there was pressure about being thin and I was a few pounds overweight. It was important to my mother, who wanted to make certain that I "looked good" to friends and family, so she would occasionally put me on a diet. Because my parents kept an eye on what I ate, being a teenager I sneaked foods, especially sweets, even though I didn't particularly like them. When I returned home for vacations during my college years, my parents would put me through an inspection to determine whether I had gained weight from the last time I had seen them. Over time, this ritual caused me to develop anxiety about going home and the fear of being judged.

To make matters worse, I felt added pressure with piano and voice lessons. My school studies were not commensurate with my abilities, and my music lessons were becoming less enjoyable due to expectations I couldn't fulfill. My Attention Deficit Hyperactivity Disorder (ADHD), as yet undiagnosed, made practicing and studying challenging. Despite the pressure, I continued my piano lessons.

Family members and teachers discovered that I had a rich, contralto voice, so they encouraged me to study voice. Every Saturday, my father drove me to Manhattan for my vocal lessons. My teacher was an older Eastern European woman, Ms. Urbacher. I studied with her for several years but was unable to overcome my fear of performing. After school, I took piano lessons once a week (paid for by my grandparents) with Miss Goodkind, a Julliard teacher who taught at a neighborhood music studio.

There were ample opportunities to play in piano recitals, sing solos in school plays or in the choir at my synagogue, where, for several years, I enjoyed a wonderful spiritual experience. My parents seemed determined that I become a music teacher (at the time it was considered one of the only professions for women), but I was unsure about teaching. I hadn't been allowed to choose or pursue other interests. It was evident to me that what I wanted for myself was less about me and more about my parents. They were caught up in the Long Island culture, and it became more important to them to boast about my accomplishments without necessarily understanding my struggles.

My home life was often chaotic. There were frequent distractions — football games playing every weekend on high volume and arguments between my parents. My dad was away on business for days at a time; his absence contributed to the chaos. I often retreated to my bedroom closet. It was my sanctuary, a place to escape family dysfunction where I came face to face with reality. I felt little self worth, overcome with guilt, my independence stifled. I was very aware of what wasn't working in my parent's relationship with me.

With the disappointments in my studies and my parents, I did experience some shining musical moments in high school. I won several awards for outstanding music achievements. One summer I was selected to be one of four alto singers in renowned choral conductor Robert Shaw's chamber choir, performing the *St. Matthew's Passion* by J. S. Bach. The program also gave me an opportunity to sing in a chorus accompanied by the Cleveland Orchestra, directed by Leonard Bernstein, performing Mahler's 2nd symphony. I was mesmerized by his conducting and his expressiveness. I'll never forget when the soprano soloist hit her highest note in the piece. It sent chills through my entire being. Another summer I performed with a chorus under the direction of Eugene Ormandy, who conducted the Philadelphia Orchestra.

I also socialized, went to friends' parties on the weekends and joined the school chorus, where I was an alto singer and piano accompanist. Saturdays were family time when I regularly visited both sets of grandparents in Brooklyn, spending the day together, sometimes meeting for dinner. I was also seeing Mark, my future husband, whom I met in 7th grade and was my salvation.

My first date with Mark, who lived three blocks away, included dinner and a Broadway show in New York City. He was very generous, escorting me to ballet performances, theatre and fine restaurants. Initially, Mark was much more serious than I. He was kind, giving, and had a wonderful family. I felt accepted in his home, especially when my family life was chaotic and unsettling. He was an anchor, helping me feel like an insider, embracing me, giving me a great sense of comfort and belonging. I longed for that connection since I continued to be plagued by guilt and lack of self-worth. It seemed that whoever I was and whatever I did it was not good enough.

I often thought about running away. My parents seemed to have no clue or self-awareness of how they behaved, no concept of what my needs were. They were wrapped up in their world where they wanted to impress friends and family. My needs were secondary, and my parents didn't have the capability to realize them.

There were some disturbing incidents that impacted me while I was in junior high and high school. It was customary that twice a year parents signed a report card with teachers' grades and comments. When I received mine and presented it to my parents, they would often act displeased with the report. The truth is that I wished I had something more stellar to present to them.

Nonetheless, they handled the situation poorly, handing the report card back and forth to each other, almost taunting me, as if I didn't feel badly enough. Eventually, but reluctantly, they signed it.

My mother was obsessed with cleanliness. In our living room, there were French chairs covered in plastic. No one was permitted to sit on them. Magazines lying on the kitchen island were removed. One day my mother found my clothes hanging over the arms of my bedroom rocking chair. She threw the clothes on the floor along with items from the six dresser drawers, even throwing some small items out the window into the backyard. She told me she would be going out for a few hours and expected me to have everything tidied up by the time she returned. The incident was very traumatic, yet it didn't change my attitude about how I would continue to keep my room.

Unfortunately, my attempts to talk to and reason with my parents — whether to relate how I felt about practicing or studying, being unhappy about dieting, wanting to pick out my own clothes, or getting a job away from home — was a never-ending, fruitless endeavor. Inevitably, it became easier to stay silent, which caused me frustration and anger.

I continued to see Mark. It was especially meaningful to be included in his family's Passover Seder with his grandfather "Poppy" Sam and his grandmother Gussie. Mark and I, his parents and cousins sat at a long table elegantly dressed with a lace cloth and formal dinnerware. Poppy Sam relished leading the service, which was quite lengthy.

I often visited Sam and Gussie's house in Atlantic Beach, where they summered, or Mark's mother's parents, David and Mary, in New York City, where Poppy David was a dentist.

At age eighteen Mark and I went separate ways to college. My father, who was raised to believe that it wasn't important for women to attend college realized that if he and my mother wanted me to become a teacher they would have to send me. I was accepted at a music conservatory that required liberal arts, with the option of earning a degree in teaching. During my college years, my mother encouraged me to continue to see Mark. My father, though, tried to shake my trust in Mark and our relationship. He declared that "men have only one thing in mind," as if he didn't recognize Mark's love and respect for me in all the years we dated. Once he realized Mark was committed to marrying me, he accepted the relationship, satisfying his own expectation that the role of women was to marry and have children.

At the age of nineteen, during one of my college breaks, I tried once again to exert my independence. One day I suggested to my parents that I spend a summer working in Boston, living in an apartment with some friends. The next morning, I was awakened by my parents standing near the doorway of my bedroom proclaiming that I was selfish to even consider leaving home. Fear and guilt overcame me and my longing for independence once again was quashed.

Dissonance *(conflict, lack of harmony)*

The year was 1964. I was a fifteen year old eighth grader sitting on a curb on a late fall day in Woodmere, New York, waiting for my mother to pick me up. As I waited, the street seemed to be especially busy, maybe because it was nearing rush hour. The sun was out, but my jacket was unable to provide the warmth needed for such a chilly day. I had just been dismissed from my piano lesson, my teacher annoyed with me for coming unprepared. She stated that "I was wasting her time and mine." This wasn't the first incident, but it was upsetting nonetheless, and I couldn't seem to break the cycle of not meeting my parents' and teacher's expectations in music and at school.

Miss Goodkind, my piano teacher, was a handsome women in her 40s, with dark short hair, medium-framed, dressed conservatively, usually wearing a simple white shirt with scarf, skirt and flats. The piano studio was one room, spacious, but sparsely furnished with a sofa, a few folding chairs, and an old black Steinway grand. Miss Goodkind taught there once a week, the other days teaching at Julliard. My mother often drove me there, but occasionally, I would take a public bus, sometimes experiencing a lump in my stomach, feeling unprepared for my lesson. I knew what the repercussions would be. My piano teacher believed in my abilities as a pianist and hoped I would be interested in concertizing one day. She tried to persuade me to take lessons with her at Julliard — if I was committed to becoming a serious student. I wasn't prepared to accept that invitation, since there were too many things standing in the way. Although I learned piano easily, I failed to properly practice for my lessons, the primary reason being my inability to focus more than one hour at a time. My teacher and my parents wanted me to be more than I could be, a music "star", but the pressures of that were too great for me to handle, the struggles too difficult.

My lessons continued to be disappointing, the frustrations and insecurities mounting. Miss Goodkind often paced the floor, staring out the window while I played. I could usually anticipate her telling me that I had not met my responsibilities, feeling like a failure. At the end of each lesson she would give me an assignment for the following week, writing in bold red letters with several exclamation points, which felt angry and aggressive. Playing the piano was becoming less enjoyable. More than once my mother threatened to stop my lessons, often throwing my music on the floor with great force. I felt anger toward my mother but knew I couldn't express it for fear of retribution.

Waiting on the curb all I could think about was my mother's reaction in finding out what happened at my lesson. I was anxious and felt incapable of success with no place to turn. Opening the car door my mother glowered at me; I felt shame and humiliation. I knew what was next. The incident would be reported to my father. The thought of him castigating me once again brought me fear and depression. I was disappointed in myself and felt hopeless.

Giocoso *(joyful)*

I finally married Mark, shy of twenty-one. It took a year and a half to plan the wedding, and I recall the back and forth difference of opinions between my parents, my in-laws and me in making the final arrangements. There was also the matter of my wedding dress, the first one I tried on being my favorite. My mother, who needed to have things her way, was not open to purchasing the first dress I saw, insisting upon shopping for myriad wedding gowns, convinced that there was something more wonderful than the gown I first chose. After exhausting all the options, we ended up with the first one.

Our June 1971 wedding, scheduled right after college graduation, was exceptional in that we had all four sets of grandparents, feeling so grateful that we could share such a joyous life event with them. It seemed as if it was a party for my parents and their friends. My parents actually took out a second mortgage to finance our splashy and formal affair. Two hundred twenty-five friends and family attended, many who I didn't know. Only one table was set aside for our friends.

The party was at the Conservative synagogue located around the corner from our home. The ceremony took place at a sanctuary teeming with magnificent flowers. Mark, donned with a tuxedo and top hat, and I, in my Juliet-style bridal gown, stood beneath the chuppah, the traditional wedding canopy. A rabbi presided over the traditional prayer service, including the seven blessings taken with wine and breaking of the glass (symbolizing destruction of the Temple in Jerusalem). The dining room was beautifully decorated with tastefully set tables, elegant dinnerware and lavish centerpieces filled with aromatic and voluminous pink and white flowers. There was a wonderful band playing the Standards, an overabundance of hot and cold delectables, and wine and champagne flowing freely. It was truly an extravagant event, one that made me feel uncomfortable, since living on Long Island made me self-conscious of how much things cost. My parents often reminded me of that, and I felt compelled, out of guilt, to thank them profusely.

It was a tradition in my husband's family to have a long honeymoon. A seven week trip to Europe was presented to us, including plane tickets, hotels and Eurail passes. I had never traveled overseas. Until then, my excursions had been limited to upstate New York and an annual trip to Florida during Easter vacation. Mark was quite comfortable being away from his friends and family having spent the summer of 1968 in Kenya working with a professor in Njoro as part of the Agricultural program at Edgerton College.

We traveled mostly by train through Switzerland, Italy, England, and Scotland, captivated by the countryside and landscape. We also visited Copenhagen, Amsterdam, Paris, and southern Sweden, enjoying the main tourist attractions. I was nervous being so far from home. I was homesick, but the experience of that trip gave me a taste for travel and the desire to see more of the world.

After our honeymoon we moved to New Haven so that I could attend the Master's program at the Yale School of Music and my husband could begin his first year at Yale Medical School. Before I applied to graduate school I asked my father for financial assistance but he declined, feeling that his responsibility for my schooling had ended. However, Yale offered me a substantial scholarship to cover most of the costs for the two year program.

My first year of married life was a big adjustment. In some ways I still didn't know what it meant to be independent. Even though my husband and I lived in Connecticut and my parents in New York, they seemed to have too strong a presence in our lives, sometimes causing strife in our marriage. I was still influenced by my parents, and was caught between my loyalties to them and Mark. During my teenage years, my parents put restrictions on me driving, working, or being away from home for more than a few weeks. I never knew what it meant to experience life as an independent thinker. There were times when I felt paralyzed making a decision. I worried how my parents would feel, not how I felt. They were still controlling me from afar; I had to break that cycle. I had become too dependent on my parents, and realized how critical it was to tackle this issue. I knew I needed therapy. My husband supported my decision to seek outside help.

There were so many obstacles to overcome: freeing myself from years of guilt, learning how to be independent. In a way I was starting my life over again, working toward becoming a stronger and more secure individual. As I progressed with my therapy, I felt freer and happier. I was ready to cut the apron strings that restricted me in my daily life.

Con Dolore *(with sadness)*

My father's father, Grandpa Morris, was a tough man inside and out. His weakness in life was his stubbornness and it became the primary cause of his death. Morris always thought that someone was out to get him. He was willing to pick a fight with a sibling, a friend or a foe. There was one disturbing incident when he stormed into my house in Long Island, very upset with my mother while she was lying in bed, unwell. I can't even remember what the argument was about, but my grandfather expressed such anger that I ran to my bedroom trembling, anxiously waiting for him to leave.

On other occasions though — when we would meet for dinner in Brooklyn for example — my grandfather would impart some wisdom or be consoling, taking on the role as a real "family man". At one of his favorite Italian restaurants, "The Carolina" located in Coney Island, where my parents, my brother and I would sit at a long table with my grandparents, uncle, aunt, and two male cousins, my grandfather was quite funny and entertaining. It was a side of him I preferred. It wasn't easy, though, being the only granddaughter, since I almost always had to be the "obedient one," tending to my grandparents' needs or acquiescing to their demands.

Despite his tough exterior, my grandfather paid for my piano lessons, supporting my interest in music. Although he was not a musician, music flourished in his household. His brothers played the piano and violin. When I was around 11 years of age, after I had been playing the piano for three years, my grandfather introduced me to Manny Hirsch, the violist who had played with Rudy in his string quartet. Until then, I knew little of Rudy, my grandfather's younger brother.

I had read the letters Grandpa Morris and Rudy wrote between 1931 and 1932. I appreciated how diametrically opposite they were and was surprised by their close and unlikely relationship. Rudy was gentle and supportive financially and emotionally; my grandfather was difficult and often on the offensive. Morris

The Gift of Rudy

Mr. Morris Fuchs.
℅ General Delivery.
Indianapolis.
Indiana.

Hollywood — June 17.

Dearest Moish: —

It is not entirely my fault that you didn't hear from me much sooner. I wanted to write you but didn't know where to write.

I didn't get your letter until June 6, and I had six shows that day and did not get a chance to wire you or Ray. I have written Ray since. I am now on vacation for a week starting today and I have just finished reading your letter and here I am answering promptly.

2.

Listen Moish, if you don't know where you're bound for, as long as you are going places, why not come to me? My job is sure for at least six more weeks and I have a little dough saved up so you don't have to worry. I need you here and you know it so if you have no place in particular to go to, come here and don't worry about anything. If you're short on jack let me know, old pal. Don't hold

3

anything from me, you son-of-a-gun. Maybe you could find something to do here. Try it, it was lucky for me. Please write soon and let me know. I don't know why you should want to go anywheres else. Write or wire as soon as you get this letter. Boy, how I would love to see you. Tomorrow will be a year since I last saw you and it certainly feels like ten years. Think it over and I hope you come here. I am feeling great and was delighted to finally know where I could get in touch with you.

I have been O.K. so your worry has been for nothing, don't ever worry about me. I have had everything a fellow could want and I hope you decide to come here, please, because you have nowheres else to go and I want you here. After all, Morris is Morris.

Love from your pal forever,
Rudi.

Thursday.

Dearest Moisha and Stella:—
Why don't you and everybody stop worrying about me? I received your letter today when I got back to work; this week happening to be my vacation.

I ~~stoped~~ laid off writing home for a few days because I knew Mom went away with Hen & Pop so nobody was home anyway. So I decided to wait awhile till they got home. Isn't that natural especially when I did not know where they were going?

Why, I am in the best of health and feel great after a nice restful week at the beach and I gained five pounds this week. Tonight we go back to work and start in on a rehearsal and open tomorrow with "Sally," Ziegfield's musical show. Listen, you know how hard it is to make money these days so why not let me collect a bunch of shekels? Don't worry, I'll be home soon enough, I guess. Orchestramen in theatres don't last very long due to new managers, chiseling & politics so it may not be long now.

I hope you and your kids and Stel and Pop & Mom & all the boys are feeling fine. I went to some fight with Albert last Friday night and he wanted to be remembered to all of you. So did Johnny and Bertie.

So now, dear brother and sister, please have patience and it may not be long before I'll be home. And I still can't see why everybody should miss me so much when the whole family is all together, thank God.

You know, all I might be able to do when I got home was sleep and help you eat. Would that be so nice? I've thought of that too, but we shall see what will happen later on. I am keeping my eyes wide open!

Well, write soon again and I am sending all my love to you, Stel, the kids, Mom & Pop, Hen, and all the rest of the family.

Always yours — Rudy.

respected and admired his younger brother, often listening to his advice. After Rudy's plane crash at the Chicago World's Fair, it was my grandfather who was called to the scene to identify him. Remarkably, Rudy's ring was found along with his train ticket at the charred site.

The year before my grandfather became ill, my husband and I shared our news about going to work for the World Health Organization in Nepal for a year. Grandpa Morris, who had traveled and lived extensively in the United States struggling to find work as a heating engineer, was the only member of my family who offered us emotional support, seeming to appreciate how our experience abroad could be meaningful. I was quite surprised by his response.

Grandpa Morris was 74 years old when he developed prostate cancer. That was not an uncommon issue at his age, and a standard procedure would have more than likely remedied his problem. But he thought he knew best and ignored the warning signs, eventually finding a doctor who reassured him that he could simply leave it alone.

Although I thought of my grandfather as a brute — he was built like a wrestler and withstood many physical challenges — his cancer spread to his bones. I visited him a few times in the hospital toward the end of his life. He was unrecognizable. It was almost impossible for me to erase the image of him jaundiced and wasting away, a man who was once so fit, vital and strong. But the thing that never left me, as he was dying, were the words of love he professed to us: sweet, tender words. I found myself in such an emotional state I had to leave the room. Why hadn't he shared those words with us more often? It was all too late. I have thought about this scene over the course of my life, because so many of us either don't take the time or don't find it important enough to express our true feelings. My grandfather never realized what he missed, the value of sharing kind words and affection with his loved ones. It was his not knowing that brought me profound sadness.

Consonance *(agreement, compatibility)*

An unexpected opportunity came along in 1973 which would transform Mark and me. Two years into our marriage, after I had graduated from music school and my husband was finishing his second year of medical school, we became aware of a World Health Organization program involving tuberculosis vaccination work in Nepal. It was an avenue for me to exert my independence, to do something adventurous; a rare moment to travel and experience the world. Mark heard a lecture at Yale presented by a student who had just returned from Nepal, describing his time there. Mark was captivated by the student's presentation and proposed that we consider working overseas for a year. It was also fortuitous that Yale had a travel fund for medical students who wanted to do research anywhere in the world between their second and third year.

My parents reacted negatively to my trip. They felt that I was being spiteful and selfish, intentionally electing to spend almost a year in a country that was so far away from them. Months before we left for Nepal my mother would make comments about Nepal's earthquakes and legalized marijuana; but nothing they could say would dissuade me from my decision to go. It was vital that I assert my independence; this was the perfect opportunity.

We bought 'round the world plane tickets. In planning the trip, we gave ourselves plenty of time before and after Nepal to see as much of the world as we could, sometimes flying to a different place every day or every other day with our backpack and sleeping bag. It also gave us time to adjust to jet lag and prepare for living in a foreign culture.

When we arrived in Kathmandu in October 1973, monsoon season was still lingering. We spent some time there to acclimatize ourselves to our new environment while waiting for the muddy roads to dry out.

Our first stop was Biratnagar, in the Terai, where it was buggy, hot and humid. We stayed there for several weeks in a stucco-type home with a British group that worked with the World Health Organization, waiting to get our orders to head to the Himalayan foothills.

Our next stop was Ilam. The ride was long and arduous. We rode in an open jeep designed for six to eight people; there were twice as many of us, in addition to multiple bags of rice and corn. The jeep followed a muddy and mountainous dirt trail. Sometimes the driver had to stop to chop down a tree to clear the way. We stopped a few times for short breaks.

Ilam, the largest town in the district, was in the Himalayan foothills. It was delightful and charming, with beautiful tea gardens surrounding the town. Every week the local farmers sold their produce in the center square. A witchcraft doctor, holding a baby under his arm, showed off his skills, twirling a plate in each hand as he balanced them with long, thin sticks.

Sometimes we ate at the local hotel in the square, sitting at a community table with dishes of dal bhat, a lentil and rice dish that the Nepalese consumed twice a day. There were several varieties of lentils, green or moong dal being the common one, and the rice was Basmati, which was quite aromatic. Utensils weren't used, so we learned to eat with our hands, requiring a certain twist of the wrist in order to scoop up the mixture with the thumbs pressed against the second and third fingers.

A British couple with their very young daughter lived in the house we were assigned. Mark and I had our own room where we slept on a wooden board that served as a bed. There was no running water and no electricity or telephone. Our shower was a metal can with holes in it that was installed on the ceiling of a downstairs closet. Water, collected from the local river, was poured from a bucket at the top floor of the house down a tube to the metal can/showerhead. The water was very cold. If we were lucky it lasted all of 30 seconds.

Drinking water was unsafe, so we boiled it over firewood placed on a clay dung mound. We added iodine to the water for brushing our teeth. There were no bathrooms, only a water closet outside that had been built especially for the British couple. The Nepalese comfortably went outside to do their business.

We had a favorite tea shop run by "Fat Didi" that we would frequent in the Bazaar, enjoying the local tea with her sweet puris (puffed breads). Besides dal bhat, our diet consisted of doy churra; home-made unpasteurized yogurt with raw pressed rice; meat, vegetables and eggs; and local fruits such as mangos, guavas, papayas and suntalas, which resembled a tangerine that had very few seeds. We often picked suntalas from trees growing on the hillside. We consumed several of them at a time to quench our thirst, not relying on water. Badam, or peanuts, a great snack food, were also plentiful.

Along the scenic foothills, we continued to take in magnificent greenery, gardens and snow-capped mountains. It was also a time to acquaint ourselves with some of the local Nepalese, a very warm and friendly people with whom we communicated in our limited Nepali. The Nepalese often liked to ask what time it was even though most of them didn't have a watch or didn't know how old they were. Their calendar revolved around the moon, which was their time keeper.

Ilam was our first base camp, a jumping off point where we journeyed to smaller villages to vaccinate. Since communication was limited, a messenger would often walk to a village a few days ahead of us, notifying the villagers that we were coming. Mark and I each trekked to a different village with our supplies carried by porters who also cooked for us and led us there. Most of the Nepalese had never seen a white woman before, so initially I experienced culture shock. Their caste system, similar to the Indian caste system, did not allow them to comprehend our way of life, confused about how to label us since we didn't fit into any particular caste. It was an ongoing dilemma.

Life was very primitive in Nepal. Most people lived in one room clay dung homes with a thatched roof. Cow dung was considered a very important resource for building, fuel and fertilizer. With few windows, and smoke always present from cooking and heating, good ventilation was almost non-existent. If one member of a family had a severe cough, it meant that he or she was probably contagious. A tuberculosis vaccination was an important preventive measure. The cure involved taking medications — often inaccessible to the Nepalese — for at least a year. Since clinics were few and far between, we would see up to 100 people a day, both young and old. Mark taught me how to vaccinate. The process required rubbing an arm with alcohol, waving a blunt needle over a flame a few times to sterilize it, injecting the needle, and then wiping the area again with alcohol. It was a crude method, but effective.

At the end of the day, with the help of a porter, I would meet Mark at the vaccination center. From there we would plan to travel to another village the following day. When the villages were far away from our home bases (Ilam or Jorsali) we would stay in the area for a few days, camping near different Nepalese homes. When we completed our work in that area we returned to our home base. No matter where we were we had to heed warnings to find shelter once the sun went down, since there was a risk of being attacked by Tibetan bandits.

Our second base camp was Jorsali, a much smaller town than Ilam. We had a painted wood house with a few rooms. One room served as both a bedroom with a wooden board for a bed and a storage area for our pots and metal dish ware. We kept the usual vaccination routine, but one day one of our plans went awry. Mark and his porter were to meet me at my vaccination village when they were finished, but after several hours they hadn't shown up. I had a moment of panic: no communication, no sense of direction, thinking it's so easy to get lost and I might not see my husband again. Fortunately, he finally appeared and it confirmed what a tricky business it was counting on things working without any means of communication.

Jorsali was also home to a special and memorable event: a wedding procession, with a bride, 12 or 13 years old, and a groom about the same age.

There were trumpeters, horn players and drummers, and lots of spectators in the square. The bride looked very unhappy and so did the groom. The custom was that once a girl menstruated, she was ready to marry, all pre-arranged. A couple was expected to have a large family with the children eventually working on the land and taking care of their animals.

Mark and I managed to get a few weeks off for vacation. Since our stipend was only thirty dollars a month for the two of us, it limited where we could travel. We decided to head to Darjeerling, but it was a challenge getting there. We hiked several miles to a rapid, bridgeless river, where we had to walk in a chain gang across treacherous waters to the other side. We waited for a bus to retrieve us, then shared a car with two Indian officers, who were carrying rifles, on a very windy, narrow, mountainous road. We finally arrived at a beautiful, former British hill station in Northern India surrounded by magnificent tea gardens. The town was out of a story book, but it was February and the hotel had no central heating. Our British-style hotel overlooked the snow-capped Himalayan mountains. We were thrilled to have a real bed with a mattress; however, the room was cold and we needed hot water bottles to warm our bed and ski jackets to use the bathroom. We also took a few days to visit Gangtok, Sikkim, an exotic place in one of the Himalayan Kingdoms where few Westerners ventured.

As a western doctor Mark was held in great esteem. He always carried a medical kit with him, offering advice and medicines to villagers who complained of ailments. I brought extra bottles of iron pills for personal use, but gave most of them away to women suffering from anemia due to a diet deficiency or worms they contracted from unsanitary conditions. We shared care packages from our parents that consisted of canned fish and chewing gum with our friends. The villagers seemed to be fascinated with gum wrappers, making chains out of the foil. Tin cans were also recycled to put knickknacks in.

The Nepalese were extremely aware of and starry-eyed about America, its wealth and prosperity. A common and innocent question often posed was,

"How long would it take to walk there?" Everyone we spoke to wanted to visit America.

Believing that all Americans were wealthy, there was an assumption that the things we brought with us, such as cameras and sleeping bags, should be shared with friends and acquaintances. At first we were taken aback, but then we realized this behavior wasn't a matter of malice or greed but a presumption that we could easily afford to replace them. We also learned that anything left out in our room was considered public property.

For most Nepalese, we were their first encounter with Westerners. Villagers were curious about us. Young children peeked through our bedroom window early in the morning. Adults watched us eating rice and lentils or getting dressed and undressed in the confines of a sleeping bag.

Our time in Nepal was filled with so many wonderful memories. It was a place innocent, untouched and undiscovered by most tourists, unchanged for a thousand years. We watched Nepalese chanting and dancing under the full moon, emitting a spiritual energy. The repetitive chant was hypnotic.

We established wonderful friendships with the Nepalese. We gazed daily at the Himalayan mountains, especially Kangchenjunga and Everest, a magical experience each time we witnessed them. We walked trails, not knowing where they led, hiked to a Tibetan village where we ate dumplings and soup, and camped out under a spectacular full moon that felt as if it was close enough to touch. We gazed at magnificent orange and pink sunsets, appreciated the luxury of an egg. Our porter ran after a chicken to slaughter and cook it for dinner. It turned out that to Nepalese every part of the chicken is a delicacy, including the beak. (The breast meat is the only part they don't consider succulent.) We walked a full day to visit an ayurvedic doctor only to discover that he wasn't there.

Returning to the States took some readjustment. Life in Nepal was so simple, while Western life was anything but. Arriving at JFK airport, my parents rejoiced in seeing us. They asked some questions about our experience, but their enthusiasm quickly faded. After a week or two, there was little or no mention of Nepal, as if that part of my life never existed. They had little interest in our time away and how it had changed and awakened us. The Nepalese had been kind and giving in contrast to my parents who failed to exhibit the warmth or understanding of my transformative year away. They thought of that time as their loss, rather than as a time when I gained knowledge, confidence and independence.

The experience of Nepal is embedded in my memory. The smells, sounds, crisp air, spectacular scenery, and the wonderful Nepalese with whom we felt a deep and mutual respect, reminded us of a year that changed our lives, gave us a greater appreciation of what we have, and the importance of giving.

Timorose *(with hesitation)*

After my time in Nepal, I taught in public school and performed vocally at local venues. I also reflected on being a mother, not convinced that I wanted children, and certainly unprepared to take on such a responsibility. A model for motherhood did not arise from my own upbringing. As I later discovered, I would be, in a sense, starting fresh, discarding mistakes from my childhood, reassessing my parental role. It would take time and psychological assistance before I could become a good parent.

It was nine years into my marriage before I decided to be a mother. I gave very careful thought to and evaluated the kind of parent I wanted to be. Unlike my experience, I desired that my children be contented, confident and secure in their lives. I felt I was finally prepared to do whatever it took to give love, care and time to my children. It was one of the most important turning points in my life and continues to be.

I have relished being a mother. I have learned so much about myself from my children. I seek to strengthen my role as a parent with awareness and honesty.

Inquieto (restless, uneasy)

With my encouragement, my parents moved to Connecticut when my father retired. I thought it would be a great opportunity for our son and daughter to have a connection to their grandparents. When the children were very young, they enjoyed having my parents at our home on weekends and for special holidays and birthday celebrations. It was a second chance for me to have a better relationship with them. As the children got older, my parents weren't as accepting of them. Either they weren't enamored with how I was raising them or they didn't fit the prototype of who their grandchildren should be. I often became a mediator, trying to keep the peace while defending my children.

After more than 20 years living in a retirement community, my parents felt the need to be in a warm climate through the winter months. They alternated residences for several years, Florida in the winter, Connecticut in the spring and summer. Eventually they moved to Florida full time.

Before their permanent departure from Connecticut, I was called upon to help my parents move. We packed up a full condo's worth of boxes, and I helped with a last minute decision to sell a sixty-year collection of stamps that was stored in an enormous cabinet in our attic. My assistance was always taken for granted. I reached a place where I finally asked my father to use the word "please" when he asked a favor. I was trying to break patterns from the past, and I felt I needed to set certain standards of expected behavior. By then I was very comfortable speaking my mind, knowing they couldn't hurt me anymore.

I was relieved when my parents moved to Florida full time. Even though many of the parameters and expectations in our relationship were established while they were living in Connecticut, I knew that I had to accept and make allowances for some behavior that wouldn't and couldn't change.

Our relationship continued with daily phone calls. Occasionally, Mark and I visited my parents in Florida, as well as other family members who lived nearby. My parents seemed happy in their surroundings, living in a community that provided them a good social life, warm weather and an array of activities.

Risoluto (bold, resolved)

Eight years ago, in 2010, I opened a closet door in my home office and gazed at a necklace that was a gift from my mother. It had been sitting on a shelf untouched for a long time. I picked it up. It seemed ugly to me. I thought that my mother had no taste, and decided to give it another home: my waste basket. I found more of my mother's mementos scattered throughout the house and they soon shared the same fate as the necklace.

In the same closet I found piles of family videos, even old 78 rpm records that had been ignored for several years. I sorted through the stacks of items and examined all of them closely to refresh my memory. Videos don't lie. I was aghast at my parents' poor behavior toward my children. After a few weeks of looking at all the photos and videos, I decided to convert everything to CDs and DVDs, labeling them for future reference.

Fermato *(firmly resolute)*

I had a well of musical ideas waiting to be released, but I needed to cleanse myself of negative childhood experiences in order to have a clear head for creating and composing. The past held too many insecurities for me. I had never had the support of my parents or teachers; they dashed my hopes for pursuing my talents, preventing me from being a free thinker. In order to face the past once more before I "let go", I decided to return to several of my former residences, family cemeteries and a Miami Beach hotel where I had once visited my grandparents

My first stop was Kingston, New York, where I lived when I was five to ten years old. The two story family house hadn't changed much, except the porch was painted blue instead of white. The neighborhood felt less quiet and rural, but the elementary school down the street where I once posed for a photo looked exactly the same. I tried to locate my first piano teacher's home but couldn't identify it, even though I knew the street where she lived.

A few months later I paid a visit to Brooklyn. My mother's parents had lived in a rent control project building near Flatbush, and before that, a second floor walk up, in a brick, three story house across from a high school. My father's parents lived on Ocean Parkway and before that, Sheepshead Bay. Included in that trip were two cemeteries, one of them containing Rudy's grave.

The same year, while on a cruise in the Caribbean, our ship docked in Miami. My husband and I rented a car to drive to an area with Art Deco buildings, one of which was an old hotel on Collins Avenue where my grandparents spent their winters. As the only granddaughter on my father's side of the family, I was expected to spend time during Easter vacation with my grandparents. It was generally an unpleasant experience because the hotel was occupied with elderly people and there wasn't much for me to do other than to be good company for my grandparents who were very controlling and difficult.

In addition to the fact that the hotel had changed its name, the neighborhood now felt unsafe. The park that once occupied space across the street was now a vacant lot. There were chains on the doors, and the first floor looked as if it was being used as a soup kitchen. The interior however, looked exactly the same. Even the white wrought iron railing leading to my grandparent's apartment was still intact.

Each of these visits helped to lift the heavy load I had been carrying since my youth. There was still work to be done; I needed to resolve the relationship between me and my parents.

Not long after the trip to Florida, I had a vivid dream about Miss Goodkind, my high school piano teacher. I felt compelled to call her, even though more than 40 years had elapsed since I last saw her. I was uncertain if she would remember me. When I phoned her, she asked if I was still pursuing my music, never mentioning my aptitude for piano but praising me for my singing voice. Checking off the list of the people, places and things that had caused me so much sadness in my past, I asked if I could visit her. She lived in the same Manhattan apartment as when I last saw her. When I rang the bell my heart raced. Miss Goodkind, 86 years old and looking remarkably well, was dressed in a dark skirt, collared shirt and flat shoes. She welcomed me in. Nothing in the apartment had changed a day. Except that I had changed; I was no longer the fearful, insecure person who had to accept what was expected of me in my career.

At the end of a pleasant visit, she handed me a book of piano exercises, insisting that I send them back to her once I had copied them. I didn't know what to make of her gesture. Was she implying that I needed to concentrate on my piano skills, since I neglected those under her tutelage, or was it just a kind offer to give me something useful for my piano studies? I left her apartment knowing that I would never view them. I was done with that part of my past, ready to move on. A few days later, I returned her piano exercises without ever copying them.

After revisiting my childhood places, cleansing my head of negative experiences, and with the aid of medication for my ADHD, I felt ready to be productive. I decided to contact Orianna Webb, a composition teacher at the Yale School of Music, to study and expand my knowledge of writing music. It was also the time that I began extensive research on my great uncle, Rudy, whose musical career aroused my interest.

My composing flourished. I completed five CDs of chamber music in five years. I thought about Miss Goodkind again. I contemplated sending my music to her so she would know what I had accomplished. Before I could mail her some CDs though, I read her obituary online.

Sonore (harmonious)

From the age of five, when I first touched the piano keys, until fifteen years ago, I never had a piano I called my own. I inherited a baby grand of mediocre quality from my Grandmother Rose and later received a second console piano from my Grandpa Harry. The two pianos remained with me for most of my life until I donated the baby grand to a club hall in our town. Soon after, I found a home for the console as well. As a serious musician ready to delve into composing, I yearned for a grand piano, an instrument that would produce beautiful tones.

After researching and testing out Japanese and Steinway pianos, I narrowed my choice to a model B Steinway (second largest grand.) The Steinway factory in Queens was having a sale, and my husband, my daughter and I ventured off one Saturday — on one of the rainiest days of the year — to check out the display of many model Bs on the floor. The place was buzzing with teachers and their students looking for the perfect piano. I tried out two or three before I came across a 1936 restored model B made in Germany. It had a glorious sound and touch. Ironically, the previous owner was Yale University, where I attended the School of Music. I asked my daughter to sit at the piano until I located a sales person, making certain I was to be the future owner of the instrument.

The model B Steinway is a powerful presence in my music room as I rediscover the joy of music that was lost to me. As I play, I frequently turn my head to gaze at the black and white framed photo of Rudy on the mantle, giving me inspiration.

Apassionato (with fervor)

After going through a year-long process of eliminating negative energies from the past it seemed I had a lifetime of musical ideas waiting to reveal themselves. I always had an interest in composing melodies. I was intrigued with music theory and the analysis of compositional structure; but there was always something getting in the way of my creativity: travel, raising a family, performing. Then, ten years ago, I finally tapped in to my "musical well". It felt good to unleash the overflowing musical ideas that would later become albums of chamber music: varied styles of pieces for quartets, solos, trios, and duets of diverse instrumentation.

It was cathartic working with a continuous stream of music for five years, composing at my beautiful new piano using Finale, a computerized notation program. A few times each day I frequent my piano room, reviewing what I have composed, making revisions to the melodies I choose to retain. Then I concentrate on those melodies that will become themes, selecting a key and instrumentation.

I have an outline or blueprint of what will be the overall structure of the piece. The next step is to enter the music into Finale. It lays out the chosen instruments on staves, the key signature and the time signature. Then I begin to fill in each part with the harmonies, structure, key changes or modulations and elements of surprise. The goal is a well-constructed piece that sounds beautiful and engages the audience.

Years ago, I composed an album *Remembrance* in Rudy's memory. It included pieces written in the style of compositions he enjoyed playing. It seemed fitting that my memoir should include a composition in honor of him. I sat at the piano for weeks, experimenting with various melodies for a two or three movement sonata for violin and piano, but it didn't feel right. I wanted a composition that would be simple, but beautiful, reminiscent of Rudy's era, the

1920s and 1930s. In trying to create a piece that included those characteristics, I often turned toward his photo on my mantel. I soon realized that a piano piece alone would not suffice. The composition needed a viola part, not one that merely harmonized with the piano part, but one that would have its own melody, thereby creating two independent melodies that blended with each other. When I was done, I entitled it *Another Time* to memorialize Rudy's life. Most important, I knew the viola part needed to be performed on Rudy's viola!

Ardore (with love and warmth)

I grew up hearing about my great uncle Rudy, his life as a brilliant and gifted violinist, and his death at the young age of 25, though in fact he was only occasionally mentioned.

In 1992, a stack of sheet music arrived at my house. It had belonged to Rudy. It was sent to me by the son of Henry, Rudy's youngest brother. Handling it with care — it was almost 100 years old and showing signs of deterioration — I leafed through it, seeing if any of the titles of the pieces were familiar to me, or if there were any of Rudy's markings or fingerings present. Surprisingly, there were very few. I found a box, put the music in it and placed it in my cabinet.

Many years later I decided to look over the music again. I recognized a familiar piece with an intricate and difficult violin passage with orchestral accompaniment. I sat down at the piano and played the violin part. Suddenly, I found myself sobbing uncontrollably. I thought about Rudy's tragedy and tried to imagine how, as a virtuoso, he would have performed this beautiful piece.

As I began to dig deeper into Rudy's past, blogging about him on my web site, I received other gifts. I began to sense there was something more

Receipt for Rudy's viola, purchased in 1923 with a deposit of $40.

connecting us beyond his story. I needed to unearth the mystery of Rudy's life and music. As a musician, I felt spiritually connected to him. But first, there were some unanswered questions: What happened to his two violins? Where were his missing recordings?

Rudy's chin rest etched with "Rudolph Fuchs 1920"

After almost three years of exploring Rudy's past, his life story was beginning to consume me. I decided, in the middle of October 2015, to take a respite. I planned an overseas trip.

In mid-December, a few weeks before departing, I received an email from a young woman who learned about Rudy on my web site. She sent me photos of her viola, asking if I thought the instrument might have belonged to my great uncle. She included a copy of the original receipt for the viola and a photo of a chin rest with Rudolph Fuchs 1920 etched in it. The timing of this extraordinary gift gave me pause. It was all the more remarkable because I had no idea that Rudy even played the viola. I was overcome with emotion and asked myself, *Who was the messenger of this instrument?* I was able to purchase the viola and I knew immediately I was meant to play it.

Earlier in my research, I learned that Rudy had made two four minute recordings in 1929 for personal use, one where he accompanied a tenor singer, and the other a violin solo of *Ave Maria*. No one in Rudy's family possessed them or was even aware of the recordings. The chances of them appearing were slim to none. I rationalized not hearing him play by telling myself that recordings in 1929 were experimental, the sound quality poor, static being a common problem. Instead, I decided that it was best to use my imagination. I longed, though, to hear Rudy perform. I was jealous of my dad who had the fortune to be in Rudy's room when he practiced.

In May 2017, my dream was realized when a record collector emailed me, confirming that he had one of Rudy's recordings, a Gounod piece for tenor with a violin accompaniment. The collector sent me a CD copy of it. A few months later, I placed a winning bid on Rudy's original record. His playing exhibited emotion, sensitivity and maturity beyond his years. I was so moved that I couldn't seem to get enough of hearing it.

A missing recording of *Ave Maria* is yet to find its way to me, its whereabouts unknown. I have reached out to record dealers in case they come across it. I must be patient if I want to experience more of my great uncle's mastery of the violin, the recording being the last important link in my continuing journey and inquiry.

Misterioso (mysterious)

I have a dream about Rudy, who appears exactly as in his photos. He is riding in the front passenger seat of our large sedan, relaxed and loquacious, exchanging words with the driver and me. It's a beautiful day, not a cloud in the sky. We're passing trees and sidewalks in what looks like a residential area, similar to the neighborhood I once lived in on Long Island. Next, we are in a spacious room sparsely furnished with a few chairs and music stands. Rudy tells me he is to be my mentor for my weekly viola lessons, as if it is his role and responsibility to teach me. I watch him extend his arm as though guiding me.

There are many ineffable energies.

I visited Rudy's cemetery a few times, the last time in 2015. It was the culmination of my research on Rudy. My husband drove me to Queens on a Friday in the fall. The Fuchs family plot was difficult to locate. It was almost 4:30 in the afternoon and the gates were about to close because of the Sabbath. The plot was one of the farthest away from the entrance, but we still had some minutes before we needed to exit the cemetery.

The grave site showed signs of neglect. Tree branches were strewn about and the grass was overgrown. My father's parents, Morris and Still, Charles's oldest son, Kenneth, and other less familiar relatives were buried there. Next to Kenneth was Rudy, his stone quite small, dwarfed by all the other gravestones. I stood there fixated on the dates engraved on the stone, 1907-1933, with sadness and disbelief. He was only 25 years old and I still mourn his death. Everything I heard and read about him over the years confirmed that he was a man of character – caring and generous, with an abundance of talent and a promising career ahead of him.

Playing Rudy's viola gives me a greater understanding and knowledge about his life. I am ready to revisit his grave, imagining that I will focus on the dates again, 1907-1933, and what few words are inscribed on the grave stone. I expect to feel an even stronger link to my great uncle, an extraordinary man who remains in my heart.

One day, brilliant sunshine poured into the small, cozy room in my house where I practice my viola. As I played my pieces, I glanced at the tall, Norway spruces outside and then turned my attention back to the music stand. Suddenly an orange light flashed through the window. It disappeared as quickly as it came. I tried to make sense of it, but it was unexplainable.

I have also been curious about the white light displayed on the wall of the music room, bright enough to illuminate a dark room. On a sunny day, the wall looks like a backdrop for a movie with shadows of fluttering leaves, a reflection of the many full-grown trees in front of our house. Sometimes I barely make out the outline of a face in the shadows on the wall. It is another ineffable event. Can it be Rudy? I can sense Rudy's presence when I play in this room or my piano room, creating an aura of contentment.

Additionally, there are two round lights on the ceiling. One in particular has been fascinating to watch. Inside that light I have witnessed something that resembles a baton stick beating in time to the music I am practicing.

There are many ineffable energies.

Fastoso y Con Amore
(proudly and with love)

Rudy's life continues to impact mine in a positive and transformative way. His achievements, determination and love of music and family are an inspiration to me. I have been given a second chance to fill my heart with the joy of music I lost during my teenage years when my teachers and parents expected too much without emotionally supporting my music and school studies.

My self-esteem and confidence are burgeoning. I attribute this transformation to my journey eight years ago, letting go of the people and things that weighed me down, along with an unexpected event: the discovery of Rudy's story and his gifts. I am convinced that this was no coincidence. The timing of the viola coming to me, my enthusiasm for playing it, and subsequently writing about the journey, was meant to be experienced and told. Writing has allowed me to uncover my deepest inner feelings, expressing my thoughts and releasing heaviness from my mind and heart.

I am undergoing a new phenomenon: the drive to succeed and play with all that I am capable of, stemming from the possession of Rudy's first instrument. Knowing that my great uncle of enormous talent once held it in his hands, playing with love and emotion, has moved me to put my soul into playing it.

I have been taking viola lessons for almost three years since October, 2015, with a wonderful teacher who validates my abilities and hard work. Having studied piano and cello most of my life, I had little hesitation about beginning a new instrument. Playing the viola fulfills me. I not only enjoy the progress I am making but appreciate the instrument's beautiful and rich tone.

My practice time continues to increase due to my enthusiasm and the demands of learning a difficult instrument. I find myself picking up the viola several times during the day, unsatisfied that I have practiced enough, hoping that the pieces will get a bit easier to play and the sound purer.

I am captivated by the viola, sometimes dreaming about it, with images of me repeatedly playing a musical passage of a piece or a scale or arpeggio to improve my technique. Reflecting on the singular dream I had about Rudy, when he comes to me with his outstretched hand and insists on being my mentor, I feel that I was meant to play his instrument.

I have never grown attached to an instrument as much as I have to Rudy's viola. Each time I practice, I try to envision how he played. I feel blessed and privileged to own it. I have both a desire and responsibility to treasure and care for it and to play with expression and love.

There is more to discover about the viola repertoire, which is not as plentiful or well-known as for other stringed instruments. Although some of the literature is advanced, I want to experience and master it no matter how long it takes.

Playing a stringed instrument takes a commitment. The goals are playing in tune; understanding how a bow helps an instrumentalist play with expression; learning how to play spiccato (when the bow bounces slightly off the string) and staccato; and learning different types of vibrato and when to use them. It is a challenge that now feels realistic rather than unattainable.

It is Rudy's story that has empowered me, helping me to realize my potential for success and achievement, offering me calm, inner peace, optimism, confidence in my writing and composing, and enabling me to establish positive relationships with family and friends. I marvel at the influence Rudy's viola has had on me, an unexpected and magnificent gift that continues to provide pleasure and delight. Now I remain open to what lies ahead....

Coda *(finale)*

For weeks I anticipated the recording of my musical composition *Another Time,* written in honor of Rudy. I felt it would add the finishing touch to this memoir.

The recording engineer, Alec, my teacher and I met on September 14, 2018, with no sense of how long it would take to record the duet with viola and piano or how the final piece would sound. Although we only rehearsed for 45 minutes before recording, Jill, my teacher for six months, and I played as if we were one. She commented that this is a rare occurrence. I was astonished how Jill made her musical entrance, producing a rich and gorgeous tone on Rudy's viola. My first thought was, *Will it ever be possible for me to reproduce the same sound?*

We finished the recording session in only four takes, an indication of how well we blended together.

After making the edits and balancing the sound of the piano and viola, the three of us discussed how the session went. We all felt Rudy's presence in the room while playing his piece. Jill expressed how this recording experience was one of her more memorable musical moments. Alec stated how well we all worked together. My heart felt full. I was thrilled with the musical performance of *Another Time,* knowing that this journey has touched my life and the lives of others. This piece brought me to tears, a reminder of what this story has meant from its inception and how it is still evolving.

An audio version of Another Time can be downloaded at *thegiftofrudy.com.*

The Soul of Music

The soul of music slumbers in the shell

'till waked and kindled by the master's spell

and feeling hearts touch them but lightly, pour

4 thousand melodies unheard before.

- Rudy Fuchs

Another Time

Sharon L Ruchman

Copyright © 2018 Sharon Ruchman
An audio version of *Another Time* can be downloaded at *thegiftofrudy.com*

Another Time

Sharon Ruchman

Another Time

Another Time

Acknowledgements

I want to give special thanks to Davyne Verstandig who has been my guide, supporter and enthusiast. Without her dedication and belief in me, this book would not have been possible.

I want to thank Orianna Webb, my composition instructor at the Yale School of Music, who gave me the confidence to complete five CDs of chamber music. I want to thank Lisa Laquidara, my first viola teacher, who taught me well and gave me a good technical foundation. I want to thank my present viola teacher, Jill Pellett Levine, who continues to inspire me, believing in my abilities as a string player, making music a joyful experience once again. Many thanks to Alec Head, a long time friend and talented recording engineer, who has beautifully mastered my five CDs and *Another Time* for this memoir; to Dan Hamilton, graphic artist, for cover art; and to Rich Pomerantz, photographer, for images of the viola, the original receipt and Rudy holding the violin.

Special thanks to Spencer Fuchs, Steve Bennett and William Bennett, sons of Rudy's brothers who have shared photos, documents, and Rudy's sheet music, invaluable information for this book. I am grateful for the wonderful relationships that have developed with these family members as a result of my journey with Rudy. I feel blessed to have continued support of my husband Mark.

Bio of Sharon Ruchman
(sharonleer@mac.com
www.sharonruchman.com)

Sharon Ruchman, a Connecticut resident, is a singer, composer, pianist, and violist. She began piano studies at the age of 8, studying with Rosetta Goodkind, a teacher at the Julliard School of Music, when she was in junior high and high school.

Sharon graduated from the New England Conservatory in 1971 where she was a voice major. While there, she accompanied the Conservatory chorus under the direction of Lorna Cooke DeVaron and conductor Seiji Ozawa.

During the summers, Sharon attended the Ambler Music Festival sponsored by the Philadelphia Orchestra and the Blossom Music Festival sponsored by the Cleveland Orchestra, where she was chosen to sing in renowned choral conductor Robert Shaw's chamber choir.

At Yale School of Music, Sharon was an alto soloist with the Yale Glee Club and New Haven chorale. She was invited to participate in the opera program at the Norfolk Music Festival in Norfolk, Connecticut.

After graduate school, Sharon taught music in the West Haven public schools. In 2007, she returned to Yale to continue her composition studies with Orianna Webb.

In 2008, she released her first chamber music CD featuring *Sea Glass*. Subsequently, she completed the following CDs: *Arrival of Spring, Remembrance, Textures, Love and Ceremony*, and *A Bit of Tango*. Sharon's *Piece for Cello and Piano* was chosen to be played in San Francisco by the National Association of Composers (NACUSA). Her piece *Day at Play and Day's End* was performed at the Women Composer's Festival in Hartford. Her compositions have also aired on WMNR and WSHU, classical radio stations in Connecticut and several radio stations throughout the U.S., Canada and Australia.

Sharon is presently studying viola with Jill Pellett Levine, a violist with the New Haven Symphony, and has created music for two children's book series *Little Brown Bear* and *Wanda Wannabee* with Susan A. Katz, teacher, author, and poet. Her resume and samples of her music can be found online at sharonruchman.com.

Bio of Rudy

1907 — Born November 6, Brooklyn, New York

1920-1923 — Played viola, his first instrument

1923 — Began to play the violin

1925 — Graduated from high school

1928-1930 — Performed as a violin soloist and member of the Vertchamp String Quartet (the first violinist, Albert Vertchamp, was his teacher) in New York City, Philadelphia, Princeton

1929 — Debuted in Steinway Hall
   Made his first two recordings for personal use

1930 — Performed for President Coolidge at the White House
   Purchased an 1837 Charles Francois Gand violin

1930-1933 — Became a concertmaster on the radio station KMTR in Los Angeles, also moonlighting for bands and orchestras on the West Coast

1931-1932 — Exchanged letters with my Grandfather Morris, whom he financially supported while Morris looked for work as a heating engineer.

1932 — Legally changed his name from Rudolph Fuchs to Rudolph Fox

1933 — Died at age 25 in a Sikorsky seaplane crash at the Chicago World's Fair, June 12

Rudy Fuchs, also known by his stage name, Rudolph Fox.

Program for a concert with Rudy and Josef Wohlmann at Steinway Concert Hall in New York.

Invitation Violin Recital
by
Rudolph Fuchs

Knabe Hall
Fifth Avenue at 39th Street

Sunday Evening, March 27th, 1927
at 8:15

Program

I

Chaconne	Vitali-Charlier

II

Concerto—F Sharp Minor	Vieuxtemps
Allegro	
Andante	
Rondo-Allegro	

III

Praeludium et Allegro	Pugnani-Kreisler
Nocturne	Chopin
Carmen Fantasia	Hubay

IV

Gypsy Serenade	Valdez
(Ampico Accompaniment Recording of Joyce Albert Vertchamp)	
Polonaise Brillante—A Major	Wieniawski

Joyce Albert Vertchamp at the Piano

KNABE-AMPICO USED

R.S.V.P.
Mrs. Albert Vertchamp
439 Fifth Avenue, New York

Invitation to a recital at Knabe Hall, March 27, 1927

Rudolph Fuchs at the Knabe Hall

Rudolph Fuchs

Before a capacity audience Rudolph Fuchs, young and talented violin artist, appeared on the 27th of March in the following program: Chaconne, Vitali-Charlier, Vieuxtemps Concerto, (F. Sharp Minor), Praeludium & Allegro, Pugnani-Kreisler, Nocturne, Chopin, Carmen Fantasia, Hubay, Gypsy Serenade, Valdez, Polonaise Brillante, Wieniawski.

Mr. Fuchs gave strong evidence of his brilliant talent in artistic playing and true interpretation. The audience received each number with warm appreciation. Joyce Albert Vertchamp presided at the piano and displayed artistic musicianship.

Rudolph Fuchs, is a young artist of only nineteen years. His remarkable musical talent and absolute command of his instrument are attracting much attention in musical circles. He was educated in New York, his entire musical training having been personally supervised by Albert Vertchamp. Before completing his school studies, several years ago, young Fuchs was chosen by Mr. Walter Damrosch as the most talented and able violinist in the schools of Greater New York, to play as concert master in an orchestra under his direction. He is engaged for concert appearances in many eastern cities. Besides this, he is second violinist in the Vertchamp String Quartet and concert master of the "Y" Symphony Orchestra.

Review in Horvath's Bulletin, April 1927

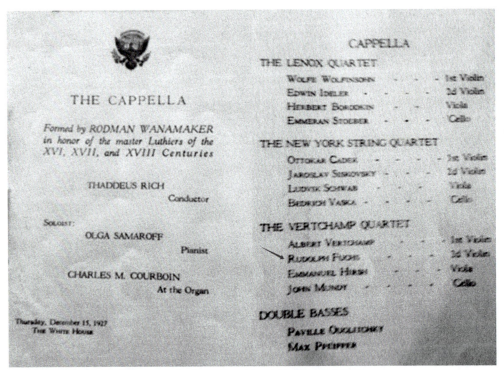

Program for a performance before President Calvin Coolidge at the White House on December 15, 1927

Announcement of Hovarth Bulletin's Debut Recital award for 1928.

Rudolph Fuchs
Swiftly Rising in his Art

Rudolph Fuchs, young violinist, and member of the Vertchamp String Quartet gave evidence already of his sobre talent and exquisite musicianship through his recital last year. We had the opportunity to observe his gradual and steady advancement on the violin, which reached a complimentary stage and became promising for the future of the young violinist.

Rudolph Fuchs

His progress and solid foundation justifies our expectation to see him very soon before the musical public as an outstanding figure in the violin playing art.

The Bulletin takes pleasure in repeatedly mentioning Mr. Fuchs to our readers and to the public.

Review in Horvath's Bulletin, October 1929

Made in the USA
Middletown, DE
24 November 2018